HOLLYWOOD WITS

HOLLYWOOD WITS

EDITED BY K. MADSEN ROTH

AVON BOOKS NEW YORK

HOLLYWOOD WITS is an original publication of Avon Books. This work has never before appeared in book form.

AVON BOOKS
A division of
The Hearst Corporation
1350 Avenue of the Americas
New York, New York 10019

Copyright © 1995 by Bill Adler Books, Inc.
Cover art by James Bennett
Published by arrangement with the editor
Library of Congress Catalog Card Number: 94-47041
ISBN: 0-380-77765-7

Library of Congress Cataloging in Publication Data:

Hollywood wits / [edited by] K. Madsen Roth.
     p.   cm.
   1. Motion picture industry—United States—Quotations, maxims, etc. 2. Motion picture actors and actresses—United States—Quotations. 3. Celebrities—United States—Quotations. I. Roth, K. Madsen.
PN1994.9.H66   1995   94-47041
791.43'0973—dc20   CIP

First Avon Books Trade Printing: August 1995

AVON TRADEMARK REG. U.S. PAT. OFF. AND IN OTHER COUNTRIES, MARCA REGISTRADA, HECHO EN U.S.A.

Printed in the U.S.A.

OPM   10 9 8 7 6 5 4 3 2 1

Contents

Out There in La-La Land

Seventy-two suburbs in search of a city.

DOROTHY PARKER, on Los Angeles

Hollywood—an emotional Detroit.

LILLIAN GISH

I'm an actor, not a star. Stars are people who live in Hollywood and have heart-shaped pools.

AL PACINO

Hollywood—that's where they give Academy Awards to Charlton Heston for acting.

Shirley Knight, on why she didn't show up for the ceremony when she was nominated for Best Supporting Actress for *Sweet Bird of Youth*

You can take all the sincerity in Hollywood, place it in the navel of a fruit fly and still have room enough for three caraway seeds and a producer's heart.

Fred Allen

A leader of public thought in Hollywood wouldn't have sufficient mental acumen anywhere else to hold down a place in a breadline.

ANITA LOOS, author of
Gentlemen Prefer Blondes

Just outside of pious Los Angeles is Hollywood, a colony of moving picture actors. Its morals are those of Port Said.

H. L. MENCKEN

California's a wonderful place to live—if you happen to be an orange.

FRED ALLEN

 5

All creative people should be required to leave California for at least three months every year.

GLORIA SWANSON

I've spent several years in Hollywood, and I still think the movie heroes are in the audience.

WILSON MIZNER, gambler,
sportsman and wit

We have our factory, which is called a stage. We make a product, we color it, we title it and we ship it out in cans.

CARY GRANT

I was born at the age of twelve on the
Metro-Goldwyn-Mayer lot.

> JUDY GARLAND, who had been
> performing on stage as Frances
> Gumm since the age of five,
> and who was actually fourteen
> when she made her first movie

Hollywood is the place where people from
Iowa mistake one another for movie stars.

> FRED ALLEN

In Hollywood, a starlet is the name for any woman under thirty who is not actively involved in a brothel.

BEN HECHT, who wrote the screenplays for *Wuthering Heights* and ALFRED HITCHCOCK'S *Notorious*

I've seen grown men throw down their coats for Dietrich to walk on; I've seen Jean Shrimpton stop traffic as she crossed a London street; and I've seen Tuesday Weld send Miss Harris's Dance Class in New York City, in 1959, into disarray as all the young gentlemen (including me) left their partners stranded on the dance floor to queue up for a few seconds in her arms.

JOHN LAHR, on glamour

There are two reasons why I'm in show business, and I'm standing on both of them.

BETTY GRABLE, whose legs
were insured by Lloyds of London

The people here even looked different—they were well dressed, confident and laid-back. They crossed the roads slowly in the wrong places, and all the cars screeched to a halt to let them go.

MICHAEL CAINE, describing
his first visit to Beverly Hills

 9

The key to getting ahead in Hollywood is *schmooze, schmooze, schmooze!* But make sure you schmooze the right people, such as the director. I once spent an hour and a half schmoozing the pool man. (I never got the part, but I had a free supply of chlorine for a year.)

JON LOVITZ, actor, writer

Include me out.

SAMUEL GOLDWYN

You're only as good as your next picture.

SAMUEL GOLDWYN

Movies are like high school with money—
everyone's absolved of responsibility, actors
in particular, and you run around behaving
like you're four.

ANTHONY LaPAGLIA

What the world needs is more geniuses
with humility. There are so few of us left.

OSCAR LEVANT

 11

There is a haste and a lack of dignity to film stardom. I do not mean to criticize. There are many stars here who have great talent. I merely say that from my own standpoint I am not at all proud because I have become a film star.

MARLENE DIETRICH, in 1934, the year she played Catherine the Great in *The Scarlet Empress*

I've done the most awful rubbish in order to have somewhere to go in the morning.

RICHARD BURTON, explaining why he was in so many bad movies

Richard and Elizabeth? I don't know any Elizabeth and Richard. Why don't people sign their last names?

GIG YOUNG, after receiving a congratulatory basket of flowers from the Burtons for winning the Best Supporting Actor award for *They Shoot Horses, Don't They?*

I was now drinking up to three bottles of vodka a day, and the trouble with doing something like that is that at the end of the day you can't count—so you don't know you are doing it.

MICHAEL CAINE

It sure got to me, that picture. And I want to tell you, after seeing that picture, I have sworn off. I am through! I will never go see another picture again as long as I live!

JOE E. LEWIS, in his nightclub act after seeing *The Lost Weekend*, the searing study of alcoholism that won four Oscars, including Best Picture

Now they're calling taking drugs an epidemic—that's 'cos white folks are doing it.

RICHARD PRYOR, who was nearly burned to death while free-basing cocaine

No drinking, very little smoking—and as for the evenings, they're just as quiet. Why, they're practically inaudible. No sound at all but the popping of California *poppies*.

ADOLPH ZUKOR, eminent producer, interviewed in Paris in the late 1920s, when moralists were calling Hollywood "Sodom by the sea"

In Burbank, there's a drive-in church called Jack-in-the-Pew. You shout your sins into the face of a plastic priest.

JOHNNY CARSON

Mistresses are more common in California—in fact, some of them are very common. It's easier for a man to conceal his mistress there because of the smog.

GROUCHO MARX

Hollywood is a sewer—with service from the Ritz-Carlton.

WILSON MIZNER

A place where they shoot too many pictures and not enough actors.

WALTER WINCHELL

Nobody's interested in sweetness and light.

HEDDA HOPPER, defending
the gossip columnist's trade

Compassion is a luxury of the affluent.

TONY RANDALL

The trouble with the rat race is that even if you win, you're still a rat.

LILY TOMLIN

No good deed goes unpunished.

CLARE BOOTHE LUCE

Things are going to get worse before they get worse.

LILY TOMLIN

Cocaine is God's way of saying you're making too much money.

ROBIN WILLIAMS

The cost of living has gone up a dollar a quart.

W.C. FIELDS, when the
federal excise tax on liquor
was raised—again

In Hollywood, if you don't have happiness, you send out for it.

REX REED

I've been rich and I've been poor; rich is better.

SOPHIE TUCKER

What contemptible scoundrel stole the cork from my lunch?

W.C. FIELDS

I don't drink. I don't like it. It makes me feel good.

OSCAR LEVANT

I feel sorry for people who don't drink, because when they get up in the morning, they're not going to feel any better all day.

FRANK SINATRA

The reason I drink is because when I'm sober I think I'm Eddie Fisher.

DEAN MARTIN

Method acting? There are quite a few methods. Mine involves a lot of talent, a glass and some cracked ice.

JOHN BARRYMORE

We have passed a lot of water since then.

SAMUEL GOLDWYN, in the
1950s, recalling the Golden
Age of the late 1930s

Look out for yourself—or they'll pee on
your grave.

LOUIS B. MAYER

You have disgraced the industry that made
and fed you. You should be tarred and
feathered and run out of Hollywood.

LOUIS B. MAYER to BILLY WILDER
for making *Sunset Boulevard*

Give the public what it wants and they'll show up.

BILLY WILDER, on the crowds that attended LOUIS B. MAYER'S funeral in 1957

Death is nature's way of saying, "Your table is ready."

ROBIN WILLIAMS

More actors have been ruined by the cry "For he's a jolly good fellow" than by all the poor roles in the world.

WILLIAM POWELL, on why he wasn't a party-going man, despite his martini-consuming role in the "Thin Man" series

In the real dark night of the soul it is
always three o'clock in the morning.

> F. SCOTT FITZGERALD, on his
> dissolute Hollywood days

If I could get my membership fee back, I'd
resign from the human race.

> FRED ALLEN

That's the house that fear built.

> HEDDA HOPPER, gossip
> columnist, describing her
> Beverly Hills home

Beverly Hills is very exclusive. For instance, their fire department won't make house calls.

MORT SAHL

I've never been poor, only broke. Being poor is a frame of mind. Being broke is only a temporary situation.

MIKE TODD, producer of
Around the World in 80 Days

This slum cost a lot of money. It should look better than an ordinary slum.

SAMUEL GOLDWYN, taking
director WILLIAM WYLER to
task for how "dirty" the set
of *Dead End* looked

When Gertrude Stein returned to New York after a short sojourn in Hollywood, somebody asked her, "What is it like—out there?" To which, with little delay and the minimum of careful thought, the sage replied, "There IS no 'there'—there."

DAVID NIVEN, explicating one of GERTRUDE STEIN's more famous remarks. (Actually, she was talking about Oakland, California.)

Look at how many ugly people there are in the world. No wonder they pay *us* so much money.

MARLENE DIETRICH

What I like about Hollywood is that one can get along by knowing two words of English—"swell" and "lousy."

VICKI BAUM,
author of *Grand Hotel*

There is another thing the grocery clerk has over the picture star. If he loses his job, he can reasonably enough hope for a better job. If a star slips, he may get another job, but you can bet it won't be a better one.

ROBERT TAYLOR, after
making the flops *Lucky Night*
and *Lady of the Tropics*. His
was to prove an up-and-down career.

A verbal contract isn't worth the paper it's printed on.

SAMUEL GOLDWYN

Hollywood money isn't money. It's congealed snow, melts in your hand, and there you are.

DOROTHY PARKER

God is love, but get it in writing.

GYPSY ROSE LEE

I sometimes worry that God has Alzheimer's and has forgotten us.

LILY TOMLIN

If it isn't the sheriff it's the finance company. I've got more attachments on me than a vacuum cleaner.

JOHN BARRYMORE, who
squandered several fortunes

The only reason I'm in Hollywood is that I don't have the moral courage to refuse the money.

MARLON BRANDO, in the 1960s

Actors like him are good, but on the whole I do not enjoy actors who seek to commune with their armpits, so to speak.

GREER GARSON, on MARLON BRANDO

I gave up being serious about making pictures about the time I made a film with Greer Garson and she took 125 takes to say no.

ROBERT MITCHUM, recalling his experience making *Desire Me*

I never said all actors are cattle. What I said was all actors should be *treated* like cattle.

ALFRED HITCHCOCK

I don't want to be normal. Who wants to be normal?

DAVID O. SELZNICK, producer
of *Gone With the Wind*

Television is an invention that permits you to be entertained in your living room by people you wouldn't have in your home.

DAVID FROST, in 1971, when
he was still more entertainer
than interviewer

Television—a medium. So called because it is neither rare nor well done.

ERNIE KOVACS

If we'd had to do in the TV series what was done in the movie—a slapdash, bam-bam bunch of jokes—we'd have run out of jokes in a hurry.

JAMES GARNER, on the 1994 movie *Maverick*, a role he had originally played on the long-running TV hit. In the movie, MEL GIBSON played the lead character and Garner co-starred as a gambler.

All over America, housewives are saying, "Honey, put on your shirt. Joan Crawford's coming over."

BOB HOPE, on the first
televised Oscar show in 1952

They're not butterflies in my stomach, they're eagles.

ROBERT VAUGHN, as he
arrived for the 1959 Oscars
when he was nominated for
Best Supporting Actor for *The
Young Philadelphians*. The winner
was HUGH GRIFFITH for *Ben-Hur*.

I'm having a "Come-and-Watch-Me-Lose-Again" party.

> THELMA RITTER, at the 1959
> Oscars, having received her
> fifth Best Supporting Actress
> nomination, for *Pillow Talk*.
> She holds the record for the
> most nominations—six—
> without a win in that category.

The security is heavy and so is the insecurity.

> MICHAEL CAINE, on attending
> the Academy Awards
> ceremonies when he was
> nominated for Best Actor for
> *Educating Rita*

Ladies and gentlemen, that was bound to happen. Just think, the only laugh that man will probably ever get is stripping and showing off his shortcomings.

DAVID NIVEN, co-host of the
1973 Oscars, commenting on
the naked man who had just
streaked across the stage

I hope to God I don't get an Oscar. It would really depress me if I did.

DUSTIN HOFFMAN, when he
got his third nomination, for *Lenny*

If anyone would like to hear it, I think I still have twenty minutes left over from a highly emotional speech I made a few years ago.

> GREER GARSON, giving out the Best Actor award in 1951, harked back to her acceptance speech for Best Actress in 1942 for *Mrs. Miniver*, which remains the longest in Academy history, lasting some twelve minutes

The Academy asks that your speech be no longer than the movie itself.

> DANNY KAYE, as Oscar host, also in 1951

What a thrill for me to fondle an envelope even in transit.

CAROL CHANNING, presenting
the Sound award in 1967,
when she was nominated for
Best Supporting Actress for
Thoroughly Modern Millie

The words "Kiss Kiss Bang Bang," which I saw on an Italian movie poster, are perhaps the briefest statement imaginable of the basic appeal of movies.

PAULINE KAEL, explaining the
title of a collection of her
movie reviews

It's the kissiest business in the world. You *have* to keep kissing people.

AVA GARDNER

I've always wanted two lives: one for the movies and one for myself.

GRETA GARBO

There are two million interesting people in New York—and only seventy-eight in Los Angeles.

NEIL SIMON

True Romance?

Dahling, how does one get laid in this dreadful place?

TALLULAH BANKHEAD, on
meeting wonder-boy producer
IRVING THALBERG during her
first visit to Hollywood in 1931

I used to be Snow White, but I drifted.

MAE WEST

Houseboys.

MAE WEST, in her seventies,
during an interview at her
home, explaining the three
young men clad only in towels
who suddenly walked through
her living room

She's been on more laps than a napkin.

WALTER WINCHELL, referring
to an unnamed starlet

We should not be afraid of sex on the
screen, so long as it avoids vulgarity.

NORMA SHEARER, about to
film a sanitized version of
EUGENE O'NEILL's *Strange
Interlude* in 1932

Edith, if no woman had ever shown her
bosom in those days, you wouldn't be here.

Director VICTOR FLEMING,
countering costume designer
EDITH HEAD's objection to
giving LUPE VELEZ cleavage
in the historical drama
The Song of the Wolf

My dear, you're sitting on it.

ALFRED HITCHCOCK, replying
to a question from ingenue
MARY ANDERSON concerning
her "best side"

Any girl can be glamorous. All you have to
do is stand still and look stupid.

Love goddess HEDY LAMARR

Oh, that. You can do that standing up. So
what?

MARILYN MONROE, when
advised that a recumbent love
scene was too sexual

It was like kissing Hitler.

> TONY CURTIS, on his famous
> love scene with MARILYN MONROE
> in *Some Like It Hot*

The girl speaks eighteen languages and
can't say no in any of them.

> DOROTHY PARKER, on regal
> beauty MERLE OBERON

I started out to be a sex fiend, but I
couldn't pass the physical.

> ROBERT MITCHUM

I did naughty things. There was a time (I was in my thirties) when I wanted to see an X-rated movie, okay? I bought a blond wig. And I got into the movie. It was boring.

ANNETTE FUNICELLO,
confessing to CONNIE CHUNG

All I can say is that when I'm trying to play serious love scenes with her, she's positioning her bottom for the best-angle shots.

STEPHEN BOYD, on the
experience of costarring with
BRIGITTE BARDOT in
The Night Heaven Fell

Warren's a teddy bear, though I used to become annoyed when the teddy bear hugs turned to bottom pinches.

SUSANNAH YORK, on filming
Kaleidoscope with WARREN BEATTY

Give a man a free hand and he'll run it all over you.

MAE WEST

I'd like to do a love scene with him just to see what all the yelling is about.

SHIRLEY MACLAINE, on her
half brother, WARREN BEATTY

In the race for love, I was scratched.

Comedienne JOAN DAVIS

The important thing in acting is to be able to laugh and cry. If I have to cry, I think of my sex life. If I have to laugh, I think of my sex life.

GLENDA JACKSON

. . . the women's movement hasn't changed my sex life at all. It wouldn't dare.

ZSA ZSA GABOR, in 1979

I don't think married people ought to be conscious of the fact that they are married. They ought to live in sin, so to speak.

> DOUGLAS FAIRBANKS JR.,
> during his marriage to
> JOAN CRAWFORD, 1929–33

Ingrid, Ingrid! Whatever got into you?

> LOUELLA PARSONS,
> on her radio show, chastising
> INGRID BERGMAN after the actress
> became pregnant by director
> ROBERTO ROSSELLINI during
> their adulterous affair

I have a steak at home; why should I go
out for a hamburger?

PAUL NEWMAN, summing up
his long marriage to JOANNE WOODWARD

The difference between sex and love is that
sex relieves tension and love causes it.

WOODY ALLEN

I've fallen in love with my horse. It's a
safer bet. We all know from my illustrious
past that I should be sticking to men with
four legs.

SHARON STONE, who
purchased the horse she rode
in *The Quick and the Dead*

Dietrich's masculinity appeals to women,
and her sexuality to men.

Critic KENNETH TYNAN

Don't even tell Chuck what it's all about
or he'll fall apart.

WILLIAM WYLER,
director of *Ben-Hur*, telling
STEPHEN BOYD to create a subtext
suggesting that his character,
Masala, and CHARLTON HESTON's
Ben-Hur had been lovers as young men

I've tried several varieties of sex. The conventional position makes me claustrophobic. And the others give me either a stiff neck or lockjaw.

TALLULAH BANKHEAD

There will be sex after death; you just won't be able to feel it.

LILY TOMLIN

My heart is pure as the driven slush.

TALLULAH BANKHEAD

You'd be surprised how much it costs to look this cheap.

DOLLY PARTON

I have a face that is a cross between two pounds of halibut and an explosion in an old clothes closet. If it isn't mobile, it's dead.

DAVID NIVEN

I said before that I am not a sexy pot.

SOPHIA LOREN, on the acting ability that brought her an Oscar for *Two Women*

I've been on a calendar, but never on time.

MARILYN MONROE

Every man I've ever known has fallen in love with Gilda and wakened with me.

RITA HAYWORTH, on the
pernicious effect of the role
that made her a major star in 1946

No one ever called me pretty when I was a little girl.

MARILYN MONROE

Losing my virginity was a career move.

MADONNA

There's a broad with a future behind her.

CONSTANCE BENNETT, sizing
up a starlet in the 1930s

It's the good girls who keep the diaries; the
bad girls never have the time.

TALLULAH BANKHEAD

Most beautiful dumb girls think they are
smart and get away with it, because other
people, on the whole, aren't much smarter.

LOUISE BROOKS, the reclusive
"lost star" of the late 1920s

She got her looks from her father. He's a
plastic surgeon.

GROUCHO MARX

Give me my golf clubs, fresh air and a
beautiful partner, and you can keep my
golf clubs and the fresh air.

JACK BENNY

A woman drove me to drink and I never
even had the courtesy to thank her.

W. C. FIELDS

At his age, he should marry me!

MAUREEN O'SULLIVAN,
reacting to the marriage of her
daughter, MIA FARROW, to
FRANK SINATRA

Hah! I always knew Frank would end up
in bed with a boy.

AVA GARDNER, on ex-
husband FRANK SINATRA's
marriage to MIA FARROW

If I had as many love affairs as I've been
given credit for, I'd be in a jar in the
Harvard Medical School.

FRANK SINATRA

I am a marvelous housekeeper. Every time
I leave a man I keep the house.

ZSA ZSA GABOR

A house is like a bed. If you're getting
along, it doesn't matter how small it is. But
if you're not getting along, it doesn't
matter how much elbow room you have.

PAUL REISER

There is one thing I would break up over,
and that is if she caught me with another
woman. I won't stand for that.

STEVE MARTIN

 57

A man in love is incomplete until he is married. Then he is finished.

ZSA ZSA GABOR

Always get married early in the morning. That way, if it doesn't work out, you haven't wasted the whole day.

MICKEY ROONEY, who has been married eight times

Looking back, I don't really know why she married me. I was a jerk, though I thought I was wonderful at the time.

BOB NEWHART, after twenty-four years of marriage to his wife, Ginny

I am having a love affair with my wife, and neither of us is cheating. That is probably a first in L.A.

JOHN DEREK, on his marriage to BO

I was madly in love with Helen Slater. I thought for sure this was the woman I'm supposed to marry—I mean, we have the same last name!

CHRISTIAN SLATER, on his
costar in his first movie,
The Legend of Billie Jean

Even now I look at her and she takes my breath away. I know it sounds strange, but prior to Kim I never liked blondes that much. I never handled relationships properly. I didn't make them important enough. Sexually I was attracted, but I couldn't commit. On the deepest, nonsexual level, I loved men far more than the women I'd been with. I found that love with her.

ALEC BALDWIN, on wife KIM BASINGER

All you need is love. And good management.

PAUL REISER

I said, "Listen, buddy, I only *play* the Terminator—you married one."

ARNOLD SCHWARZENEGGER,
on what he said to TOM ARNOLD

I dress for women, and undress for men.

ANGIE DICKINSON

Chivalry is the art of lying magnificently.

BEN HECHT, top screenwriter
for forty years

Many a man has fallen in love with a girl
in a light so dim he would not have chosen
a suit by it.

MAURICE CHEVALIER

She's descended from a long line her
mother listened to.

GYPSY ROSE LEE, on a 1940s starlet

You can lead actresses to water and drink,
but you can't make them wear what they
don't want to.

EDITH HEAD, nine-time Oscar
winner for her costumes

I certainly agree with all those who find more sex appeal in Barbara Stanwyck and her ankle bracelet in *Double Indemnity* than in all those naked bodies rolling around on the screen today.

BETTE DAVIS

The idea of suggesting undress has always been more seductive than stark nakedness. The haughtiest lady in pictures or any place else is more sex-alluring when slightly covered and *suggesting* her possibilities than [when] enticing *sans raiment*. There is always that piquing idea of wondering "What has she?" Much more intriguing than "That's all there is—there isn't any more."

ROBERT KALLOCK, Columbia
Pictures designer during the 1930s

My nose. It's truly lovely.

JAMIE LEE CURTIS,
on her best feature

In this town, a girl better be ready for anything, from something that sweeps her off her feet to something that knocks her on her ass.

MARISA TOMEI,
Best Supporting Actress for
My Cousin Vinny

Looks fade, but humor is forever—I'll take Woody Allen over Warren Beatty any day.

BETTE MIDLER

I always knew something wonderful would happen to me after sixty-five.

> VINCENT PRICE, on his
> marriage to British actress
> CORAL BROWN

I sexy-ed her up in 1952's *Singin' in the Rain*, for which she has always been grateful.

> GENE KELLY, on CYD CHARISSE

I make an entrance in *Exit to Eden* that is probably the best entrance I will ever get. I'm wearing one of my dominatrix outfits: a gold bra with metal cups—big cleavage— a black satin corset and emerald-jeweled garter belt, a jeweled gold hip belt, fishnet stockings, and green satin high heels. I'm sitting sidesaddle on my horse and I ride up to a tent where the new slaves—the "citizens"—are. They are there to pay homage to me . . .

DANA DELANY

I was a horny kid. I fantasized a lot about female vampires.

JIM CARREY, of *Dumb and Dumber*, on his youth

It's not gooey. It's not like we fell in love—it's because we keep landing in each other's laps, so to speak.

Sandra Bullock, on the romantic aspects of *Speed* with costar Keanu Reeves

I've been involved in scenes in bathtubs and bedrooms and on kitchen tables, but I never even feel comfortable when I have to take my shirt off. That scene in *Dances With Wolves* where I was naked—that was in the book, to show his vulnerability and how comfortable he felt being alone. I found the biggest reeds I could to hide behind.

Kevin Costner

I just don't feel that my algebra teacher
should ever know what my butt looks like.

> JULIA ROBERTS, on why she
> won't do nude scenes

I look like a duck.

> MICHELLE PFEIFFER

Please don't retouch my wrinkles; it took
me so long to earn them.

> ANNA MAGNANI, who didn't
> want the studio stills for
> *The Rose Tattoo* airbrushed

They used to photograph Shirley Temple through gauze. They should photograph me through linoleum.

> TALLULAH BANKHEAD, while
> making *Die! Die! My Darling!*

I'm sorry, Greer, I'm ten years *older*.

> JOE RUTTENBERG, MGM
> cameraman, to GREER GARSON
> when she complained
> that he wasn't photographing
> her as well as he used to

When you're working with an actor who is married and you're married, you no longer invest anything in the kiss. When you're not married and your partner isn't married, *then* you might enter into some serious lip-locking.

JAMIE LEE CURTIS, on kissing
ARNOLD SCHWARZENEGGER
in *True Lies*

There's something very special about what's under that pot, let me assure you.

NICOLE KIDMAN, on her
husband, TOM CRUISE, and
his strategically placed kitchen
pot in *Far and Away*

Nic just makes me feel fun around her. She makes me laugh. The littlest things she'll do will get to me.

TOM CRUISE, on wife NICOLE KIDMAN

We spent a lot of time together. I mean, despite his looks, I actually did enjoy his company.

SARAH JESSICA PARKER,
on heartthrob ANTONIO BANDERAS

How do you photograph a girl so she does not appear pregnant? She can stand behind a piano.

> EDITH HEAD, on costuming a pregnant VERONICA LAKE for *Sullivan's Travels*, in which the actress spent half the movie disguised as a boy

If pregnancy were a book, they would cut the last two chapters.

> NORA EPHRON

A blow is dealt to mother love from which
that sentiment may never recover.

Time magazine, reviewing *Psycho*

It is said that life begins when the fetus
can exist apart from its mother. By this
definition, many people are legally dead.

JAY LENO

I'm going to marry a Jewish woman. I like
the idea of getting up on Sunday morning
and going to the deli.

MICHAEL J. FOX

The main result of feminism has been the Dutch Treat.

NORA EPHRON

I wasn't as uninhibited as Stuart, but I was as shocking. I couldn't get a girl to do my laundry for sex—I tried, don't get me wrong.

STEPHEN BALDWIN, on the difference between himself and the character he played in *Threesome*

A devotion to *Gunga Din* is an awkward thing to bring to a marriage. This has been particularly true since some Americans began to take movies seriously—I put the date of that sometime in the spring of 1956—and your favorite movie became less like your favorite ice-cream flavor than like a test of your character. When my wife and I got married, in 1965, I wouldn't have been surprised to hear that her friends were speculating about how long she'd be able to remain in a union with somebody who was filmically stunted.

CALVIN TRILLIN, on the CARY GRANT/DOUGLAS FAIRBANKS JR. adventure classic

Fame! Money! Ego!

When I see myself on the screen, I am so beautiful I jump for joy.

MARIA MONTEZ, who made
her debut in *The Invisible Woman*

I can hold a note as long as the Chase National Bank.

ETHEL MERMAN

I'll never forget the night I brought my Oscar home and Tony took one look at it and I knew my marriage was over.

SHELLEY WINTERS,
on husband ANTHONY FRANCIOSA's
reaction to her first Oscar,
for *The Diary of Anne Frank*

A lot of people don't like to look at themselves on the screen. But I've got an ego you can't fit in this room. So, since I love myself so much, I can tolerate even the worst work.

DANNY DEVITO

No one is completely unhappy at the failure of his best friend.

GROUCHO MARX

The worst part of success is trying to find someone who is happy for you.

BETTE MIDLER

I got what I have now through knowing the right time to tell terrible people to go to hell.

LESLIE CARON

"Thank goodness I don't have to act with you anymore."

"I didn't know you ever had, darling."

KATHARINE HEPBURN to
JOHN BARRYMORE as the end
of production neared on her
first movie, *A Bill of Divorcement*,
and John's quick retort

Bette likes to scream and yell and I just sit and knit. During *Baby Jane* I knitted a scarf from Hollywood to Malibu.

> JOAN CRAWFORD, on working with BETTE DAVIS on *Whatever Happened to Baby Jane?* Although she and Davis loathed each other, director ROBERT ALDRICH insisted there was no trouble on the set. Davis just called him every night and complained.

It's a spot I wouldn't have given to my dry cleaner.

> PETER LAWFORD, on turning down the role in *Whatever Happened to Baby Jane?* played by newcomer VICTOR BUONO, who got a Supporting Actor nomination for his performance

The older one gets in this profession, the more people there are with whom one would never work again.

LIV ULLMANN

I have known many actors and actresses. Some of them were good and some of them were bad, but among the good ones I often found many despicable traits, and among the worst, fine qualities.

Director JOSEF VON STERNBERG

When I started out, I didn't have any desire to be an actress or learn how to act. I just wanted to be famous.

KATHARINE HEPBURN

Look, I'm not a natural-born director. Now that I'm actually doing it, I wonder why everyone wants to in the first place. You have to think of *everything*.

DIANE KEATON, while directing her first studio feature, *Unstrung Heroes*

It's like meeting God without dying.

DOROTHY PARKER, on ORSON WELLES

Oh, no, he's not. God is the most important, and the governor of California is second.

SHIRLEY TEMPLE, who had just been introduced to writer H. G. WELLS and informed that he was the most important person in the world

Didn't you ask her who was third?

Studio head DARRYL F. ZANUCK, on being
told of SHIRLEY TEMPLE's ranking system

Long before she was born, I tried to
influence her future life by association with
music, art and natural beauty. Perhaps this
prenatal preparation helped make Shirley
what she is today.

SHIRLEY TEMPLE's mother

I arrived in Hollywood without having my
nose fixed, my teeth capped or my name
changed. That is very gratifying to me.

BARBRA STREISAND

I've enjoyed that I've lasted ten years, and I've made fourteen or fifteen movies in that period of time, been nominated twice for an Academy Award. And won. I like that. I like looking around and seeing lots of people who look like me, 'cause when I came out looking like me, nobody was around.

WHOOPI GOLDBERG, in 1994

She just wants to be loved, to have a family—and the house, the dog, the cars, the money, the jewelry, the clothes, y'know?

DREW BARRYMORE,
describing the murderous
home-wrecker she played in
Poison Ivy

I had no disagreement with Barbra Streisand. I was merely exasperated at her tendency to be a complete megalomaniac.

> WALTER MATTHAU, on the experience of filming *Hello, Dolly!*

Where does she find them?

> DOROTHY PARKER, on being told that CLARE BOOTHE LUCE, the acerbic author of *The Women*, was always kind to her inferiors

Egotism—usually just a case of mistaken nonentity.

> BARBARA STANWYCK

It's a great help for a man to be in love
with himself. For an actor, however, it is
absolutely essential.

ROBERT MORLEY

You can pick out the actors by the glazed
look that comes into their eyes when the
conversation wanders away from
themselves.

MICHAEL WILDING,
the British actor and ELIZABETH
TAYLOR's second husband

One thing's for sure—I hate talking about
myself.

BARBRA STREISAND

I want to live a quiet, pseudo-intellectual life and go out and direct a picture two times a year.

BURT REYNOLDS

You're always a little disappointing in person because you can't be the edited essence of yourself.

MEL BROOKS, on the
drawbacks of talk-show appearances

The secret to staying young is to live honestly, eat slowly and lie about your age.

LUCILLE BALL

Gandhi was everything the members of the Academy would like to be: moral, tan and thin.

JOE MORGENSTERN, producer

Money is the aphrodisiac which fate brings you to cloak the pain of living.

WILLIAM POWELL, when he was making one *Thin Man* picture after another

It's amazing how healing money can be.

DOLLY PARTON, after the residuals started pouring in from WHITNEY HOUSTON's recording of Dolly's old song "I Will Always Love You" for *The Bodyguard*, written after an affair went sour

It's a lousy thing for a movie star to be running out of money.

WALTER MATTHAU

I would say if you're going to get rich with Disney, you don't ask for a better salary. You buy stock.

JAMES EARL JONES, after doing the voice of Mufasa in *The Lion King*

One of the more unfortunate phases of a screen star's life is that it is easier to drive a famished cat away from a saucer of cream than to check the wagging tongue of the cat's two-legged sister in Hollywood.

CONSTANCE BENNETT,
responding to rumors of her
divorce. The marriage lasted
another year.

Even now I feel furious with myself because, whenever there's a still camera pointed towards me, my MGM training makes me smile.

LESLIE CARON, on how hard
it is to get over being a movie star

It's just beginning to dawn on me that I will never actually play for the Dallas Cowboys.

TOMMY LEE JONES, on his new box-office clout in 1994

A celebrity is a person who works hard all his life to become well known, then wears dark glasses to avoid being recognized.

FRED ALLEN

A fan club is a group of people who tell an actor he is not alone in the way he feels about himself.

JACK CARSON

Pictures are the only business where you can sit out front and applaud yourself.

WILL ROGERS, when asked
why he left the stage for movies

My wife is a woman of great taste. She has seen very, very few of my movies.

BORIS KARLOFF

What's a cult? It just means not enough people to make a minority.

ROBERT ALTMAN, on being
called a cult director

I'm an introvert. I don't want to be
famous.

> GEORGE LUCAS, who gave up
> directing for producing and
> special-effects development

A celebrity is any well-known TV or movie
star who looks like he spends more than
two hours on his hair.

> STEVE MARTIN

I never forget a face, but in your case I'll
make an exception.

> GROUCHO MARX, when
> accosted by a man who
> claimed to know him

I adore not being me. I'm not very good at being me. That's why I adore acting so much.

DEBORAH KERR, six-time nominee for Best Actress, on the attraction of her profession

I'd hate to disappoint people. I'd hate to tell people I'm not haunted by the ghost of my father. I'd hate to tell people that I live in a really nice place and intend to live there for many years to come.

DANIEL DAY-LEWIS, on why he's so secretive

All the bullwhip stories about me and Daniel are true.

EMMA THOMPSON, answering
a question for DANIEL DAY-
LEWIS at a joint publicity
appearance for *In the Name of the Father*

I have ten commandments. The first nine are, thou shalt not bore. The tenth is, thou shalt have right of final cut.

BILLY WILDER

Dear World: I am leaving you because I am bored, I am leaving you with your worries in this sweet cesspool.

> Suicide note left by GEORGE SANDERS, April 25, 1972

I don't remember anybody's name. Why do you think the "dahling" thing started?

> ZSA ZSA GABOR, onetime wife of GEORGE SANDERS

This goes to a nice guy. I've known him all my life.

> IRVING BERLIN was the presenter of the Oscar for Best Song of 1942, and discovered that he'd won it himself for "White Christmas"

I would like to thank my colleagues—
Brahms, Bach, Beethoven, Richard Strauss . . .

> DIMITRI TIOMPKIN was extremely
> annoyed that this line, as he
> accepted his Oscar for Best Score
> for *The High and the Mighty*, got a
> laugh. He was serious.

We've been doing this for years. We even
dubbed Rin-Tin-Tin.

> JACK WARNER, on the fuss over
> the fact that AUDREY HEPBURN's
> singing in *My Fair Lady* was
> dubbed by MARNI NIXON. It in
> fact was caused by Warner's
> decision not to use the show's
> Broadway star, JULIE ANDREWS,
> who swept in and won the Best
> Actress Oscar anyway, for the
> same year's *Mary Poppins*.

Nobody can be exactly like me. Sometimes even I have trouble doing it.

TALLULAH BANKHEAD,
on being impersonated

You can tune in safely—she's not on tonight!

DAVID LETTERMAN, in the
promo for his show the day
after MADONNA spouted
nonstop obscenities at him

I never go out unless I look like Joan Crawford the movie star. If you want to see the girl next door, go next door.

JOAN CRAWFORD, sometimes
called, behind her back,
"The Painted Lady"

I lived in a fantasy world in order to survive. Now that I'm here, I plan to work at it. That means playing the part—long, tight dresses, slick! Unless you rise to the occasion, Hollywood doesn't really exist.

THERESA RANDLE, of *Malcolm X* and *Beverly Hills Cop III*

I didn't go out of my way to get into this movie stuff. I think of myself as a writer.

SAM SHEPARD

Two members of my profession who are not urgently needed by my profession, Mr. Ronald Reagan and Mr. George Murphy, entered politics, and they've done extremely well. Since there has been no reciprocal tendency in the other direction, it suggests to me that our job is still more difficult than their new one.

PETER USTINOV

I know a lot of actors who have terrible lives filled with drugs, alcoholism, deception, betrayal and broken relationships. All they really care about is the life they live on the screen, and for that they get it together. But that's all they care about.

ALEC BALDWIN

Look, there are no secrets. Sometimes you walk along the beach looking for a piece of sand. Sometimes it's right in front of you. You don't have to dig. The sand is the sand—do you know what I'm saying?

TOM CRUISE, who says his life is an open beach

You go through my garbage and hide in my plants. It's not what grown-ups should do for a living.

CHER, to tabloid snoops

I'm in a very non-newsworthy place in my life, though you couldn't tell by the papers.

JULIA ROBERTS

The New York phone book has five Ruth Gordons. Not so many in Los Angeles. I wish my mother had let me take Fentress Serene Kerlin for my stage name. I bet there'd be only one of those.

RUTH GORDON

She's listed in the membership list of the Directors Guild as Irving Lupino.

JOSEPH L. MANKIEWICZ,
introducing IDA LUPINO in
1952, when she was the only
woman who regularly directed movies

If *To Have and Have Not* has established Lauren Bacall as "The Look," then *Lost Weekend* should certainly bring Mr. Milland renown as "The Kidney."

BILLY WILDER, being
lighthearted about his searing
movie in which RAY MILLAND
played an alcoholic

When my time comes, just skin me and put me up there on Trigger, just as though nothing had ever changed.

ROY ROGERS, who had his
famous horse, Trigger, stuffed
and mounted

I amended the actor's cliché to "never work with children, animals or Denholm Elliott."

GABRIEL BYRNE,
after costarring with the great
character actor in *Defense of the Realm*

I'd rather ride down the street on a camel than give what is sometimes called an in-depth interview. I'd rather ride down the street on a camel nude. In a snowstorm. Backward.

WARREN BEATTY

I really liked Lassie, but that horse Flicka was a nasty animal with a terrible disposition. All the Flickas—all six of them—were awful.

RODDY McDOWALL, on his
childhood "friend"

I had a ball, and it was just short enough not to be boring. It came back in a flash how boring moviemaking is—you know, you work for one minute and then sit around for three hours. I don't think I could do that for three months.

ELIZABETH TAYLOR, on her
return to the screen in *The Flintstones*

The physical labor actors have to do
wouldn't tax an embryo.

NEIL SIMON

All they ever did for me at MGM was
change my leading man and the water in
my pool.

ESTHER WILLIAMS

Wet, she's a star. Dry, she ain't.

FANNY BRICE, on ESTHER WILLIAMS

If you want a place in the sun, you have to expect a few blisters.

> LORETTA YOUNG, on the
> price of stardom

There used to be a me, but I had it surgically removed.

> PETER SELLERS, famous for
> his multiple roles in such
> films as *Dr. Strangelove* and *Lolita*

Acting with Harvey is like acting by yourself—only worse.

> JANE FONDA, on LAURENCE HARVEY,
> her costar in *A Walk on the Wild Side*

There is not enough money in Hollywood
to lure me into making another picture
with Joan Crawford. And I like money.

STERLING HAYDEN, who
costarred with Crawford in
Johnny Guitar, a production
legendary for its personal feuds

I have my standards. They may be low,
but I have them.

BETTE MIDLER

I know my films upset people. I *want* to upset people.

Director KEN RUSSELL

I called myself "King of Comedy," a solemn and foolish title if ever there was one, but I was a harassed monarch. I worried most of the time. It was only in the evenings that I laughed.

MACK SENNETT

Mother of three—10, 11, and 15—divorcee.
American. Thirty years' experience as an
actress in motion pictures. Mobile and
more affable than rumor would have it.
Wants steady employment in Hollywood
(has had Broadway). Bette Davis c/o
Martin Baum. GAC. References on
request.

BETTE DAVIS placed this ad
in *Variety* a month before the
opening of *Whatever
Happened to Baby Jane?*, a
movie which revived her
career and brought her her
tenth nomination for Best Actress

I used to go to Palm Springs all the time, until it got to be so fashionable. Why, you might just as well stay in Hollywood as go down there nowadays.

BETTE DAVIS, in 1936

My kids came to Austria for *The Three Musketeers*. I'd take my six-year-old and my seventeen-year-old, and we'd go out and pillage together.

KIEFER SUTHERLAND, trying to explain that it was with his daughter and stepdaughter, not CHARLIE SHEEN, that he went out carousing while making that movie

There was one more thing to do before I left London and that was to attend the premiere of *Alfie*. This time the premiere was a giant affair held at the Plaza Cinema in Piccadilly and everyone, but *everyone*, was there. All four Beatles came and all four Rolling Stones, plus Barbra Streisand and her current husband, Elliott Gould. I sat next to Tippi Hedren, who fainted at the abortion sequence in the film and had to be carried out.

MICHAEL CAINE

Miss Davis was glamorous, years ago, for about a month. This period ended when, backed up by a smart town car containing a white poodle and liveried chauffeur, and attired in moody black velvet slacks and jacket, she met her mother, who had been on a trip East, at the Los Angeles railway station. Mrs. Davis was unable to believe her own eyes and flatly said so. The glamour was dropped later that day.

JANET FLANNER, on BETTE DAVIS

A successful man is one who makes more money than his wife can spend. A successful woman is one who can find such a man.

LANA TURNER

 115

When you're down and out something always turns up—and it's usually the noses of your friends.

ORSON WELLES

France is a place where the money falls apart in your hands but you can't tear the toilet paper.

BILLY WILDER

Keep a diary and one day it'll keep you.

MAE WEST

I'm very frightened of my computer. I got a computer expert to come to my home and weed out all the options. Now I just have On, Off, Save, and Print. If I see another option come up, I'll feel like weeping.

Mia Farrow, on the trials of writing her post-Woody Allen autobiography

I haven't read any of the autobiographies about me.

Elizabeth Taylor

You can imagine what a trip this is for a Jewish girl from Great Neck—I get to win an Academy Award and meet Elizabeth Taylor at the same time.

> JULIA PHILLIPS, producer of
> *The Sting*, after receiving
> 1973's Best Picture Oscar
> from Taylor

You'll Never Eat Lunch in This Town Again.

> Title of JULIA PHILLIPS's
> autobiography recounting her
> fall from grace in Hollywood

In the
Realms
of Art

In the beginning, the movies were rude, the audience was rude, and movie art developed in an atmosphere of exhilarating freedom.

Film critic DAVID DENBY

In the year 2024 the most important thing which the cinema will have helped in a large way to accomplish will be that of eliminating from the face of the civilized world all armed conflict.

D. W. GRIFFITH, predicting
the future of movies, in 1924

In the language of screen comedians, four of the main grades of laugh are the titter, the yowl, the belly laugh and the boffo.

JAMES AGEE, the much-admired film critic, in 1949

Motion pictures need dialogue as much as Beethoven symphonies need lyrics.

CHARLIE CHAPLIN, who held out against "talking pictures" longer than anyone, refusing to use spoken dialogue as late as 1936's *Modern Times*, but finally giving in with *The Great Dictator* in 1940

Firsthand and reliable reports from the scene present a terrifying picture. Perceiving the advent of the Film Which Talks Like a Man, hundreds of movie stars who have attained their eminence because of a dimple in the chin or a bovine eye, but whose speaking voices could hardly be counted on to put across the sale of a pack of Fatimas in a night club, are now frantically trying to train their larynxes into some sort of gentility.

ROBERT BENCHLEY, in 1928,
on the advent of sound

All I need to make a comedy is a park, a policeman and a pretty girl.

CHARLIE CHAPLIN

Imagine their delighted surprise when I read them the script of *Love and Death*, with its plot that went from war to political assassination, ending with the death of its hero caused by a cruel trick of God. Never having witnessed eight film executives go into cardiac arrest simultaneously, I was quite amused.

WOODY ALLEN, on the initial
reaction to his comedy about
the Russian Revolution

No one ever went broke in Hollywood underestimating the intelligence of the public.

Legendary hostess ELSA MAXWELL

The length of a film should be directly related to the endurance of the human bladder.

ALFRED HITCHCOCK, whose
longest movie, *North by
Northwest*, ran 135 minutes

If my fanny squirms, it's bad. If my fanny doesn't squirm, it's good.

HARRY COHN, founder of
Columbia Pictures

Is it a sequel to *The Hurricane*?

GRACIE ALLEN, curious about
a movie called *Gone With the Wind*

 125

All I want to see is the horror picture to
end all horror pictures. It should be called
Frankenstein Meets Mickey Rooney. And I
don't care how it comes out.

AN ANONYMOUS MGM PRODUCER

Coming Soon! Ibsen's *A Doll's House*.
Bring the Kids!

Sign on a movie marquee
in Ohio in 1973

How about the pictures this year? Sex, persecution, adultery, cannibalism—we'll get those kids away from those TV sets yet.

> BOB HOPE, hosting the Oscars in 1959, when such pictures as *Anatomy of a Murder, Ben-Hur, Room at the Top*, and *Suddenly Last Summer* were vying for awards

Glorious Fun! Cyclonic Action! Doug Gives This Little Girl a Hand! Sock! Right On the Nose. 'Cause Our Mary's a Mean Mama, and Doug's Taming Her! A Riot of Fun—Ending With a Tender Romance.

> Small town marquee advertising MARY PICKFORD and husband DOUGLAS FAIRBANKS in *The Taming of the Shrew*

I guess you'll get the part in the school play.

> GENE HACKMAN, to eleven-year-old ANNA PAQUIN, after presenting her with the Oscar for Best Supporting Actress for *The Piano*

Goddamn little brat. You've ruined every one of my birthdays. They bring you out from behind the wallpaper to sing that song, and it's a pain in the ass.

> CLARK GABLE, complaining to JUDY GARLAND about the song "Dear Mr. Gable," otherwise known as "You Made Me Love You," which Judy sang in *Broadway Melody of 1938*

I'm so used to the new guy now, I can hardly remember what the old guy was like . . . I feel a little bit more mature or in control of—well, in control of absolutely nothing, really.

> CHRISTIAN SLATER, in 1994,
> talking about the wild days
> he'd put behind him

The embarrassing thing is that the salad dressing is outgrossing my films.

> PAUL NEWMAN

My whole life is a movie. It's just that there are no dissolves. I have to live every agonizing moment of it. My life needs editing.

> MORT SAHL

I'd love to sell out completely. It's just that nobody has been willing to buy.

Director JOHN WATERS

In *8½*, Fellini steals from everybody, just like Shakespeare.

DWIGHT MACDONALD, who
actually liked this movie

In California, you lose a point off your I.Q. every year.

TRUMAN CAPOTE

Miss Dennis acts, from beginning to end, demented, but demented in the most simperingly phony way, so that the always tenuous line between the worst kind of Method acting and raving madness disappears altogether.

Critic JOHN SIMON,
on SANDY DENNIS's performance in
Who's Afraid of Virginia Woolf?,
for which she won the
Best Supporting Actress Oscar

Pictures make me look like a twelve-year-old boy who flunked his body-building course.

JULIE HARRIS, at the time she
made *The Member of the Wedding*

I don't act. I react.

JIMMY STEWART

Elizabeth Taylor was famous, at least in legend, for never reading an entire script, just her own lines. No one's had a more fabulous career; maybe she knew something the rest of us didn't.

WILLIAM GOLDMAN, Oscar-winning screenwriter of *Butch Cassidy and the Sundance Kid*

Acting is all about honesty. If you can fake that, you've got it made.

GEORGE BURNS

Memorize your lines and don't bump into the furniture.

SPENCER TRACY

She knew nothing about camera tricks. She just turned it on—and everything else on the stage stopped.

FRANK CAPRA, on BARBARA STANWYCK,
whom he directed in several movies,
most notably *Meet John Doe*

I kept the same suit for six years—and the same dialogue. We just changed the title of the picture and the leading lady.

> ROBERT MITCHUM, on his late-1940s and early-1950s roles in such movies as *Out of the Past, The Big Steal* and *His Kind of Woman*

This is just a personal opinion, but I don't think any other star got to deliver so many memorable lines of dialogue as Bogart. With Gary Cooper we think "Yup." Gable got the famous "Frankly, my dear, I don't give a damn." Brando had "I could have been a contender," and Tracy—I can't come up with a single line to associate with that great actor.

> WILLIAM GOLDMAN

I wasn't driven to acting by an inner compulsion. I was running away from the sporting goods business.

PAUL NEWMAN

Until you're known in my business as a monster, you're not a STAR.

BETTE DAVIS

This guy Charlton Heston is a nice fellow, but what a hamola.

ALDO RAY

I accept this very gratefully for keeping my mouth shut. I think I'll do it again.

> JANE WYMAN, giving one of
> the shortest acceptance
> speeches in Oscar history after
> winning the Best Actress
> award for *Johnny Belinda*

Having no talent is no longer enough.

> GORE VIDAL, on the death of
> the studio star system

All you could see of me in the picture was the back of my head. Unless they give some special award for acting with one's back to the camera, I don't see how I could have won.

WENDY HILLER, astonished at winning the Best Supporting Actress Oscar for *Separate Tables*. Her best scene had been taken away from her and rewritten for the character played by RITA HAYWORTH.

Acting is the most minor of gifts and not a very high-class way to earn a living. After all, Shirley Temple could do it at age four.

KATHARINE HEPBURN

In *Casablanca*, there was often nothing in my face. But the audience put into my face what they thought I was giving.

INGRID BERGMAN

When she walks on screen and says hello, people ask, "Who wrote that wonderful line of dialogue?"

LEO MCCAREY, on INGRID BERGMAN, whom he directed in *The Bells of St. Mary's*

Once you were an MGM star that's the way it was. It helped to have talent, of course, but that constant saturation created this legendary kind of thing. We couldn't help becoming legends.

MYRNA LOY

Everybody wants to be Cary Grant. Even I want to be Cary Grant.

CARY GRANT, born Archibald Leach

I'm just a lucky slob from Ohio who happened to be in the right place at the right time.

CLARK GABLE

So I said to Bogey, we are going to try an interesting thing. You are about the most insolent man on the screen, and I'm going to make this girl a little more insolent than you are.

HOWARD HAWKS, telling
HUMPHREY BOGART what he
was planning to do with
newcomer LAUREN BACALL in
To Have and Have Not

Now, I don't know a lot about these things, but I have a feeling you could be a big star. I don't know about Britain, but you could be something in the States. Now, if you can talk Dostoyevsky and look like a truck driver, you've got it made. Speak one thing, look another.

ROBERT HENDERSON,
British stage actor,
to SEAN CONNERY
at the start of Connery's
career, when he was one of
the sailors in *South Pacific* on
the London stage

My kids won't think I'm just another bum.
Now they'll know what I do for a living.

> ANTHONY QUINN, on the
> importance of his first
> Supporting Actor Oscar,
> for *Viva Zapata!*

I'm going to take it home and design a
dress for it.

> EDITH HEAD, on her Black-
> and-White Costume Design
> Oscar for *Roman Holiday*

How in hell would you like to have been in this business as long as I and have one of your kids win an Oscar before you do?

> HENRY FONDA, on daughter JANE's Best Actress win for *Klute* in 1971. Nominated only for *The Grapes of Wrath* in 1940, he was finally chosen Best Actor in 1981 for *On Golden Pond*, just weeks before his death.

The only honest way to find the best actor would be to let everybody play Hamlet and let the best man win. Of course, you'd get some pretty funny Hamlets that way.

HUMPHREY BOGART, on choosing a Best Actor before the awards for 1951, when he won for *The African Queen*. His competition was MARLON BRANDO for *A Streetcar Named Desire*, MONTGOMERY CLIFT for *A Place in the Sun*, ARTHUR KENNEDY for *Bright Victory* and FREDERIC MARCH for *Death of a Salesman*. Later, many critics would lament that Brando never played Hamlet.

There is all the difference in the world between playing a character more than a thousand times, as I did, and getting your lines on the set in the morning and having to face the cameras with them in the afternoon.

SHIRLEY BOOTH, who won the
Best Actress Oscar for *Come
Back, Little Sheba*, for which
she had already won
Broadway's Tony Award

I've never been in style, so I can't go out of style.

LILLIAN GISH, who became a
star with her first movie, *Birth
of a Nation*, in 1914, and
remained magical to her last,
1987's *The Whales of August*

Working with Bette [Davis] isn't easy, but she's worth it. She's honest and outspoken. She's one of the very few actresses I know who can look in the mirror and tell herself the truth.

ORRY-KELLY, chief designer
at Warner Brothers in the 1930s

What the hell do you do with a woman that has shoulders as broad as Joan Crawford's? Take this new fashion of pads, make them even bigger and set a fashion with them.

WALTER PLUNKETT,
on fellow designer ADRIAN's
brilliant success in costuming Crawford

Not even Garbo in the Orient has approached, for special effects, Dietrich in Spain. With fringe, lace, sequins, carnations, chenille, nets, embroideries, and shawls, Miss Dietrich is hung, wrapped, draped, swathed, festooned . . .

VARIETY, on Dietrich's
appearance in *Devil Is a Woman*

You couldn't dress Billie Burke without ruffles. Even if it was a tailored suit, you had to put ruffles on it.

WALTER PLUNKETT, costume
designer at RKO and MGM,
on the beloved actress best
remembered as Glinda in
The Wizard of Oz

[Mae West] can take a dress with fur on the bottom and walk across the room when a lot of people would break their necks.

EDITH HEAD, on Mae's ability to control a costume

If you aren't pretty, make no attempt to be pretty. Be ever so smart. France remains the fashion center of the world because her women, unable to depend upon their looks, use their brains and do interesting things with their appearance.

Famous designer ADRIAN

Elsa Lanchester was rolled into two miles of linen; she had to be carried around the studio and fed through a tube.

Margaret J. Bailey,
describing Lanchester's costuming
for *Bride of Frankenstein*

But above all—actresses are not mannequins displaying gowns. The gowns are there to display the actress.

Gloria Swanson

It's either the makeup man's department or
the hairdresser's.

ALFRED HITCHCOCK,
responding to a complaint
during the filming of *Lifeboat*
that star TALLULAH BANKHEAD
wasn't wearing panties

I grew a beard for Nero, in *Quo Vadis*, but
Metro-Goldwyn-Mayer thought it didn't
look real, so I had to wear a false one.

PETER USTINOV

Loretta Young used to get the petticoats—
without paying for them—from period
dresses, and she gave them to her mother,
who was a decorator and who used to make
lampshades out of them.

Costume designer GWEN WAKELING

Hardest thing in the world is to do
nothing, and he does it marvelously.

DON SIEGEL, on CLINT EASTWOOD,
whom he directed in
Two Mules for Sister Sara,
The Beguiled and *Dirty Harry*

I'm from the let's-pretend school of acting.

HARRISON FORD, on why he
was so at home in the role of
Indiana Jones

No one was more unreal and stylized. Yet
there is no moment when he was not true.

ORSON WELLES, on JAMES CAGNEY's
unique acting style

I have this theory that all our big stars
have big heads. Have you ever noticed
that? Bogart—huge head. Jim Cagney—big
head. Nicholson—gigantic head. Meryl
Streep—big head. You can go on and on.

BILLY CRYSTAL

Development Hell. I first read the term in a movie trade publication. Finally, I had a name for what I, as a producer, had been mired in for the last twenty years.

In Hollywood, "development" is the word used to describe the process of rewriting by which movies are often never made, or, if made, sometimes bear little resemblance to the book, play, or screenplay on which they are supposed to be based.

DAVID BROWN,
who produced, among many others,
the megahits *The Sting* and *Jaws*

My own ambition as a boy was to retire.
That ambition has never changed.

GEORGE SANDERS, who made
more than one hundred films

Acting I love. You get to be psychotic and
get paid for it.

ROSIE PEREZ

Personally, I loathe tricky effects, photographing
through the fireplace from the viewpoint of a
piece of coal, or traveling with an actor through
a hotel lobby as though escorting him on a
bycicle; to me they are facile and obvious.

CHARLIE CHAPLIN, whose use
of the camera, for all his
genius, was found humdrum
by many critics

Several tons of dynamite are used in this picture—none of it under the right people.

JAMES AGEE, reviewing *Tycoon*, which starred the unlikely combination of JOHN WAYNE, SIR CEDRIC HARDWICKE and JUDITH ANDERSON, not to mention LARAINE DAY and ANTHONY QUINN

Irving Thalberg once told me that you can't always be right, but you can always be busy. No one's judgment is infallible, but it isn't the mistakes you make that down you, it's the inaction.

MARY PICKFORD, in 1933, while making her last movie, *Secrets*, only the fifth she had filmed since 1927

Acting is a job, like carpentry or building roads. There are a hundred people involved in putting you up there on the screen. The trouble with a lot of stars is that they develop heads as big as their close-ups. If I wore hats, I think you'd find I still take the same size.

SEAN CONNERY, denying
reports that his great success
in the first two James Bond
pictures had swelled his head

Once I had a terrible fight with Jack Warner, who asked me what I thought of a picture I had done with Humphrey Bogart. I told him I didn't go to see it. Mr. Warner was furious. I said that I only got paid for making pictures. If he wanted me to see them, he'd have to pay me extra.

PETER LORRE, referring to
Passage to Marseilles, one of
five films he made with Bogart

Men used to be much smaller. If I ever found a cache of 1880s men's suits in a 44-long, I'd think I'd died and gone to heaven.

HELEN UFFNER, whose collection of genuine period costumes has been used in more than 130 movies

Historically, people with big muscles only get as far as playing Hercules. I didn't expect to go as far as I have.

ARNOLD SCHWARZENEGGER

Sean said yes. In the movie business, "yes" is hedged round with "buts" and "maybes." Not so Connery. He stayed at my side. When the going got tough, he got stronger.

JOHN BOORMAN, on SEAN CONNERY, whom he directed in *Zardoz*

I've always hated that damn James Bond. I'd like to kill him.

SEAN CONNERY

If you play too many cameos, people begin to think you're in every film that comes up and they get sick of you.

SIR JOHN GIELGUD, who was
offered endless small parts
after his Oscar for Best
Supporting Actor in *Arthur*

I feel just like the Queen Mother, because I have this association with Hollywood but no function there anymore. I'm just like her. Only not as rich.

SUE MENGERS, Hollywood
superagent from the late 1960s
to the early 1980s, on what it
feels like to be out of the loop in 1994

Maybe I'd say to myself, Speed it up a little.

JIMMY STEWART, when asked
if there was anything he'd
change if he had his career over again

Someday I'd like a part where I can lean my elbow against a mantelpiece and have a cocktail.

CHARLES BRONSON

I go around grubby all the time. I just don't have the patience, except when I'm working, to put on makeup or look good.

CHER

She [Mabel Norman] weighed and hefted the pastry in her right palm, considered it benevolently, balanced herself on the balls of her feet, went into a windup like a big-league pitcher and threw. Motion picture history, millions of dollars and a million laughs hung on her arm as the custard wobbled in a true curve and splashed with a dull explosion on Ben Turpin's face.

Director MACK SENNETT,
on the throwing of the first
silent-movie custard pie,
MABEL NORMAN's inspired
spur-of-the-moment idea

The Sound of Mucus.

CHRISTOPHER PLUMMER,
referred to *The Sound of
Music*, in which he played
Captain von Trapp, by this
satirical title—until he actually
saw it and was much
impressed by its beauty

We do not want now and we shall never
want the human voice with our films.

Director D. W. GRIFFITH, in 1924

Yes, but what about the deaf ones?

> KATHARINE HEPBURN, while
> making *The African Queen*,
> after being told that the
> alligators in the river she was
> supposed to shoot a scene in
> would be frightened off by gunfire

What are you gonna do, talk the alien to death?

> JAMES CAMERON's reply to
> his star SIGOURNEY WEAVER's
> misgivings about using guns in *Aliens*

He ended up a drunk living in Van Nuys.

> BRUCE DAVISON, on what
> happened to Ben, his
> costarring rat in *Willard*

Criticizing *Jurassic Park* is like criticizing a roller coaster for not being Proust.

> Director JAMES CAMERON

I first read it and I thought, "Oh, I don't know if I can do this." It struck me as so . . . popular. Everything I had ever done had had the stench of art to it, one way or another.

> JOHN MALKOVICH,
> on *In the Line of Fire*

 165

There's another Indiana Jones script. But it's only been in the works for a year and a half—the last script took five years until everybody was happy.

HARRISON FORD, in 1993

There are a hundred rules for being a hero. Never blink your eyes when you shoot . . . If you want to show power or anger convincingly, never move your head when you say your lines. John Wayne never moved his head.

ARNOLD SCHWARZENEGGER

Every picture we make is intended to be a Big picture. We feel when we start that it will be a knockout—and we strain every nerve to make it a hit. But in creative work it simply can't be done and never will be done. If out of sixty pictures we get six or seven big hits, we pat ourselves on the back. If out of these hits we get two or three knockouts, you can't hold us.

SAMUEL GOLDWYN, in his
annual message to his
employees in 1921

Look, I know there are articles about how underappreciated I am, how I'm not a big enough star. I've read them. But I *feel* appreciated. I'm having a *great* career. I'm getting paid a lot of money. I'm getting a variety of roles. I'm doing what I want to do. What's the problem?

JEFF BRIDGES

I made some mistakes in drama. I thought drama was when the actor cried. But drama is when the audience cries.

FRANK CAPRA

The interesting thing about working for Roger was that it was not like the rest of Hollywood: women had an equal chance to do anything. It was complete equal-opportunity exploitation.

GALE ANNE HURD,
producer of *Aliens* and the
"Terminator" movies, on her
first mentor, B-picture king
ROGER CORMAN

I was afraid people would say, as some of them did say about both *Empire of the Sun* and *The Color Purple*, you know, "Oh, that's the wrong shoe size. And it's the wrong style. What's he doing? Who does he wanna be like? Who's he trying to become—Woody? Or is he trying to become David Lean? Is he trying to become Marty Scorsese? Who does he think he is?"

STEVEN SPIELBERG, on
audience expectations for
Schindler's List

I could tell you the criticism backward and forward about *Little Man Tate*. But it didn't bother me as long as they were talking about the work and not about "she has fat thighs" or something. But I fared really well with *Tate*, so I shouldn't be complaining.

JODIE FOSTER, on her first directorial effort

Critics can't even make music by rubbing their back legs together.

MEL BROOKS

A good review from the critics is just
another stay of execution.

DUSTIN HOFFMAN

They search for ages for the wrong word,
which, to give them credit, they eventually
find.

PETER USTINOV, on the critics

They released a big study about how bad
movie-theater popcorn is for you. In fact,
we went to the movies last night. The
popcorn came in three sizes: medium, large
and "Roger Ebert Tub of Death."

JAY LENO

The fact is that I am quite happy at a movie, even a bad movie. Other people, so I have read, treasure memorable moments in their lives.

WALKER PERCY, in his novel
The Moviegoer

My movies were the kind they show in prisons and airplanes, because nobody can leave.

BURT REYNOLDS, on one of the troughs in his up-and-down career

She is pretty bad, but not bad enough to be remembered always.

> ALEXANDER WOOLLCOTT,
> the irascible New York critic
> who was the model for
> *The Man Who Came to Dinner*,
> on THEDA BARA's performance
> in *Cleopatra*

I am never quite sure if I am one of cinema's elder statesmen or just the oldest whore on the block.

> JOSEPH L. MANKIEWICZ, who
> won double Academy Awards
> for writing and directing
> *A Letter to Three Wives* and
> *All About Eve*, also directed the
> far less estimable *Cleopatra*,
> starring ELIZABETH TAYLOR
> and RICHARD BURTON

I just don't know what the hell he's after.

FRANK CAPRA, on the movies
of INGMAR BERGMAN

. . . this is part of a theory I once
elaborated with Hitchcock in a happy
moment. We decided that in order to have
a sweeping success in all the highbrow
cinemas of the Anglo-Saxon world we
should make a picture about nothing, in no
language at all and with bad photography—
but copiously subtitled. We agreed that
people would scream their heads off in
delight.

ORSON WELLES, on "art
house" movies

If you have a message, send it by Western Union.

Humphrey Bogart

The only "ism" Hollywood really believes in is plagiarism.

Dorothy Parker

It Can't Be Done. But Here It Is.

Sign hanging in the office of
the superintendent of construction
at MGM in the 1930s

I want to make *The Grace Metalious Story*.
She wrote *Peyton Place*, became rich,
bought Cadillacs and killed herself. That's
a great American story.

JOHN WATERS, director of
Hairspray and *Serial Mom*

"Virgin" and "Pregnant."

The two words director OTTO
PREMINGER refused to remove
from the screenplay of his
1953 film *The Moon Is Blue*,
causing it to be denied a
Production Code seal of
approval. It was also banned
in Boston and was, of course, a hit.

Sir, have you ever considered sending your wife to the dry cleaners?

ALFRED HITCHCOCK's reply to a man who wrote complaining that after seeing *Psycho*, his wife was afraid to shower *or* bathe

Jose Ferrer, you're too good an actor to have to stoop that low.

BEA LILLIE, the great English comedienne, on Ferrer's Oscar-nominated performance as Toulouse-Lautrec in *Moulin Rouge*

A variety show including everyone at
Paramount who was not overseas, in hiding
or out to lunch.

JAMES AGEE, reviewing
Star Spangled Rhythm in 1942

It seems to be impossible for this Christian
Civilization to make a decent movie about
the life of its founder.

DWIGHT MACDONALD,
reviewing *The Greatest Story Ever Told*

Nobody Knows Anything.

WILLIAM GOLDMAN's
summation of the commercial
wisdom of Hollywood

If Truth
Be Told

Sometimes I'm so sweet even I can't stand it.

JULIE ANDREWS

Sandy Dennis has made an acting style out of postnasal drip.

PAULINE KAEL, film critic

Great beauties are infrequently great actresses—simply because they don't need to be.

GARSON KANIN

All the good things in this film were made by me. The things that are no good in it were made by others.

Director ERICH VON
STROHEIM, in 1955,
introducing a showing of his
1926 silent film *The Merry Widow*

When I started making films I wanted to make Frank Capra pictures.

JOHN CASSAVETES,
actor/director

I'm never going to be a Meryl Streep. But then, she'll never be a Dolly Parton, either.

DOLLY PARTON

When I went to school I was so smart, my teacher was in my class for five years.

GRACIE ALLEN

People don't credit me with much of a brain, so why should I disillusion them?

SYLVESTER STALLONE, who wrote the screenplay for 1976's Best Picture, *Rocky*, and refused to sell it unless he was given the starring role

When I was born I was so surprised, I
didn't talk for a year and a half.

GRACIE ALLEN

He is an excellent director's dummy. He
has no personality of his own, only an
appearance, and for that reason he is an
almost perfect actor for the fictional screen.

GRAHAM GREENE, novelist,
screenwriter and movie critic,
on the great success of
RONALD COLEMAN

John Travolta is an extraordinary young performer—part colt, part garage hand, half Achilles, half heel—a kind of centaur of the street corners.

ALAN BRIEN, British critic,
on *Saturday Night Fever*

Keir Dullea and gone tomorrow.

NOEL COWARD, on the star
of *2001: A Space Odyssey*

I can never recognize him from one movie to the next, so I never know who he is. To me he's just an invisible man. He doesn't exist.

TRUMAN CAPOTE,
on ROBERT DENIRO

The Russians love Brooke Shields because her eyebrows remind them of Leonid Brezhnev.

ROBIN WILLIAMS

His ears make him look like a taxicab with both doors open.

HOWARD HUGHES,
on CLARK GABLE

Is she fat? Her favorite food is seconds.

JOAN RIVERS,
on ELIZABETH TAYLOR

Joanne Woodward is setting the cause of Hollywood glamour back twenty years.

> JOAN CRAWFORD, upon
> learning that Ms. Woodward
> had made her own dress for
> the 1957 Oscar ceremonies, at
> which she won the Best
> Actress award for *The Three
> Faces of Eve*

It's the only movie I ever saw in which the male lead's tits were bigger than the female's.

> GROUCHO MARX, on CECIL B. DEMILLE's
> epic *Samson and Delilah*, starring
> VICTOR MATURE and HEDY LAMARR

Putting a surtax on bodybuilders. I think this is unfair.

ARNOLD SCHWARZENEGGER,
on 1993 tax increases

I never miss a Liv Ullmann musical.

BETTE MIDLER, on the
disastrous musical version of
Lost Horizon

Phyllis Diller had so many face-lifts there's nothing left in her shoes.

BOB HOPE

For the same price I can get an actor with two eyes.

HARRY COHN, the head of
Columbia Pictures, on
auditioning Peter Falk in 1958

I tended to relate to Clint Eastwood. I wanted to get roles like he got.

EMMA THOMPSON, on the
start of her movie career

Every actor who spoke English knew that role and wanted it. The people who came down to audition for that role, with their makeup men—famous, famous actors— would astound you. It was one of those unexpected things that happen that I got it. There's just no explaining it.

F. MURRAY ABRAHAM,
on being cast as Salieri in
Amadeus, for which he won
Best Actor

For one thing, I've learned how easy it is to get into a really bad movie.

DANA CARVEY, on
Opportunity Knocks

 191

I want to go until they have to shoot me.

BARBARA STANWYCK,
who won an Emmy as Best Actress
for *The Thorn Birds* at age 76.
She played a woman
passionately in love
with a priest.

So little time, so little to do.

OSCAR LEVANT

Paint eyeballs on my eyelids and I'll
sleepwalk through any picture.

ROBERT MITCHUM, who
always pretends he doesn't
take acting seriously

I have a face that looks like an elephant's behind. It would stop a sundial.

CHARLES LAUGHTON

They had to put a hitch on my upper lip to get me to smear paint all over my contour. Even that could not disguise this old, homely pan of mine.

WILL ROGERS, on being made
up for his first movie,
Laughing Bill Hyde

We didn't have a lot of mirrors when I was growing up. We had one mirror, a cracked mirror. You know, in my mind's eye I'm beautiful and tall and thin and glamorous.

The "divine" BETTE MIDLER

Here lies Paul Newman, who died a failure because his eyes turned brown.

PAUL NEWMAN, who got very
tired early on with the endless
blather about his blue eyes

I was a little intimidated at first, 'cause she's kind of a living legend, and plus, she's got her own scent.

JOHN GOODMAN, on working
with ELIZABETH TAYLOR in
The Flintstones

I often stand in a stadium full of people
and ask myself the same question, "How in
hell did I end up here?"

STING, rock star and actor, in
a commencement address at
the Berklee College of Music
in Boston, 1994

I'll never forget how horrified Fred was
when I notified him that Ginger was going
to play the part of a titled English lady in
The Gay Divorcee.

PANDRO S. BERMAN,
who produced the Astaire-Rogers
pictures *The Gay Divorcee* and *Top Hat*

I'm just a hoofer with a spare set of tails.

FRED ASTAIRE

The greatest dancer in the world ... You
see a little of Astaire in everybody's
dancing—a pause here, a move there. It
was all Astaire originally.

GEORGE BALANCHINE

Can't act. Slightly bald. Can dance a little.

Anonymous studio verdict on
FRED ASTAIRE's original
screen test in 1933

Working with her is like being hit over the head with a valentine.

CHRISTOPHER PLUMMER,
on playing opposite JULIE
ANDREWS in *The Sound of Music*

The nicest thing I can say about Frances Farmer is that she is unbearable.

WILLIAM WYLER,
who directed the mentally troubled
actress in *Come and Get It*.
There was so much trouble on
the set that HOWARD HAWKS took over.

I am just too much.

BETTE DAVIS

They'll miss me like an old monument—
like the Flatiron Building.

KATHARINE HEPBURN,
in 1967, making noises about
retirement following the death
of SPENCER TRACY and the
release of their last picture together,
Guess Who's Coming to Dinner?

Myrna Loy! What a joy!

LILLIAN GISH

You always knew where you were with
Errol—he always let you down.

DAVID NIVEN, on his great
friend ERROL FLYNN

I will show the world what a big horse you
are.

YUL BRYNNER, to INGRID BERGMAN
when she suggested he stand on
something to make him as tall as
she was when filming *Anastasia*.
Ingrid was extremely amused
at the insult.

I get a kick out of movie stars.

> JACK NICHOLSON—after he'd
> become one himself

He was the most sensitive man I've ever
known. If somebody kicked a dog a mile
away, he'd feel it.

> EDWARD DMYTRYK, on
> MONTGOMERY CLIFT, whom
> he directed in *Raintree County*
> and *The Young Lions*

I'm a student of violence because I'm a
student of the human heart.

> SAM PECKINPAH, director of
> such violent hits as *The Wild Bunch*

Woody is at two with nature.

DICK CAVETT,
on WOODY ALLEN

Actors often behave like children and so
we're taken for children. I want to be
grown up.

JEREMY IRONS

She's Ethel Barrymore at six!

ADOLPHE MENJOU,
on SHIRLEY TEMPLE's talents
when they made *Little Miss Marker*

It was no great tragedy being Judy Garland's daughter. I had tremendously interesting childhood years—except that they had little to do with being a child.

LIZA MINNELLI

Are you against stealing? Not me. It helped me through some hungry days. Anyone who's flush enough to leave a dime on the bureau wouldn't miss it, and a dime paid for a bowl of Child's vegetable soup. Why would I be against stealing? Always leave a quarter on your bureau—the price of soup's gone up.

RUTH GORDON

I've got a lot of things to do, and I don't have time to be classified as difficult.

KIM BASINGER, before she lost
a $5 million lawsuit against
her for dropping out of
Boxing Helena

I bear no grudges. I have a mind that retains nothing.

BETTE MIDLER

I knew Doris Day before she was a virgin.

OSCAR LEVANT

We're getting closer together as we get older, but there would be a slight problem of temperament. In fact, it would be bigger than Hiroshima.

> JOAN FONTAINE, on her
> tempestuous relationship with
> her sister, OLIVIA DE HAVILLAND,
> which really got rocky when
> Joan won for Best Actress for *Suspicion*,
> beating out Olivia, who was
> nominated for *Hold Back the Dawn*

What is it to be a nice guy? To be nothing, that's what. A big fat zero with a smile for everybody.

> KIRK DOUGLAS

The only thing about my life is the length of it. If I had to live my life again, I'd make all the same mistakes, only sooner.

TALLULAH BANKHEAD

Just imagine what you could accomplish if you tried celibacy.

SHIRLEY MACLAINE, on the
Oscar telecast for 1978, to her
half-brother, WARREN BEATTY,
who had four personal nominations
for *Heaven Can Wait*

People keep asking me, "What evil lurks in you to play such bad characters?" There is no evil. I just wear tight underwear.

DENNIS HOPPER

Old Cary Grant fine. How you?

> CARY GRANT supposedly sent
> this reply to a telegram asking
> "How old Cary Grant?"

One of the most beloved illiterates this
country has ever known.

> CARL SANDBERG,
> on GARY COOPER

I was a twerp if ever there was one.

> SIR LAURENCE OLIVIER,
> on his early film career

I'm a change of pace from the previous hosts. The Academy wanted someone completely devoid of humor.

LAURENCE OLIVIER, one of six hosts, including BOB HOPE and JERRY LEWIS, for the 1958 Academy Awards

I've been around ten years—a very long flash in the pan. More like a kitchen fire.

WHOOPI GOLDBERG, shortly before hosting the 1993 Academy Awards

I'm no actor, and I have sixty-four pictures
to prove it.

VICTOR MATURE, once known
as "The Hunk"

[Irene Dunn] opened the envelope and,
after an interminable pause, read out my
name. There was a roar. I didn't wait to
diagnose whether it was a roar of approval
or rage.

DAVID NIVEN, on winning the
Best Actor Oscar for
Separate Tables

My wife's in the car already. She's taking no chances on a recount.

BRODERICK CRAWFORD, after winning Best Actor Oscar for *All the King's Men*

I'm still waiting for God to tell me, "What do you think you're doing? You go back to Port Talbot. This is a mistake. We meant *Thomkins*, not Hopkins."

ANTHONY HOPKINS, after winning the 1992 Best Actor Oscar for *Silence of the Lambs*

Thank God, now we can all relax. Susie finally got what she's been chasing for twenty years.

> WALTER WANGER, on SUSAN HAYWARD's Oscar win for *I Want to Live!* (1958), which he produced. He also produced 1947's *Smash-Up*, which brought Hayward her first Best Actress nomination

They cheered me when I walked in. I'm very well known there.

> EILEEN HECKART, describing the reaction when she walked into the unemployment bureau after winning the Best Supporting Actress Oscar for *Butterflies Are Free*

I don't deserve this, but then, I have
arthritis and I don't deserve that, either.

JACK BENNY, accepting an award

I'll put it on a shelf in my living room—
one that's low to the ground so Oscar
doesn't turn into a weapon during the next
quake.

HOLLY HUNTER, on how
she'll display her Best Actress
Oscar for *The Piano*

Then we took it back to L.A. because we had to get it engraved. My assistant was carrying it in, like, a gym bag, and she put it through the conveyor belt at the airport and the buzzers went off. So this very sweet Indian woman took it out of the bag and had no idea what the hell it was. She looked at it and went, "You been working out with this?"

MARISA TOMEI, on her adventure with her Best Supporting Actress Oscar for *My Cousin Vinny*

Listen, okay, as an interview, I'm terrible. I don't have any good quotes. It's like, you know, I have no verbal skills, none. If you really want a good interview, talk to someone like Jack Nicholson. Words just whoosh out of his mouth. But me, nothing, I mean, hey, really, okay, jeez, understand?

DIANE KEATON,
on being interviewed

You see, there's an industry of rats and informants and people who make things up because of all these gossip shows. Once you have an industry in place, you have the problem. And it permeates to where it can debilitate things as important as the presidency of the United States.

JACK NICHOLSON, in 1994,
being interviewed

It's as if people have sat down and said, "Now, we've got to make these women stronger. They have to be ballsy and sassy today." So all the women are sassy and ballsy while they're being captured and sassy and ballsy while being rescued, but in fact the shape of their destinies is exactly the same.

EMMA THOMPSON,
on women's roles, in 1994

Where can *I* get a stick of dynamite?

> CARY GRANT whispered this into the ear of HAROLD RUSSELL backstage after the veteran with hooks for hands won the Best Supporting Actor Oscar for *The Best Years of Our Lives*. Russell regarded it as the greatest compliment he ever received.

The trouble with telling a good story is that it inevitably reminds the other fellow of a dull one.

SID CAESAR

A pun is the lowest form of humor—when you don't think of it first.

OSCAR LEVANT

Hanging is too good for a man who makes puns; he should be drawn and quoted.

FRED ALLEN

Do you ever give yourself the creeps, luv?

ELIZABETH TAYLOR, to
husband RICHARD BURTON
during an interview

My whole career has been devoted to keeping people from knowing me.

LON CHANEY,
"the man with a thousand faces"

I don't make jokes. I just watch the government and report the facts.

WILL ROGERS

I became an actor by accident; I'm a businessman by design.

JAMES GARNER, who has
made a lot of money in oil
and real estate

It's a strange thing, this television. God
didn't design anyone to be recognized by
two billion people.

PETER FALK,
on the worldwide success of "Columbo"

It's much harder than making a movie.
This is me having to control two hundred
irate New Yorkers and the people on our
panel.

RICKI LAKE,
on being a talk-show host

You're standing up there at the end of the show, and you might have bombed that night, but you just wave and smile and say, "I'm not Manson, I'm just trying to get a laugh." And then you're back next week.

MARTIN SHORT, on why
television is easier than movies

We had this [TV] show called "The Million Dollar Movie," and they used to show a movie twice a day, five days a week. The week they showed *Stage Door* I was the sickest little boy—I stayed home and watched it ten times.

HARVEY FIERSTEIN,
on playing hooky and
formative influences

Like most Catholic boys, I wanted to be Jesus Christ. I could never get the turn-the-other-cheek thing down, though.

JIM CARREY

I wanted to dance like the guy on the street. People here didn't like it—especially at MGM. But Louis B. Mayer was more interested in his racehorses when I came out here, which was lucky for me.

GENE KELLY

If my film makes one more person miserable, I've done my job.

WOODY ALLEN, on his movie
*Everything You Always Wanted
to Know About Sex, But Were
Afraid to Ask*

My dear boy, you look absolutely awful.
Why don't you try *acting*? It's so much
easier.

> SIR LAURENCE OLIVIER,
> to DUSTIN HOFFMAN when the
> latter showed up one day on
> the set of *Marathon Man*
> exhausted from his
> "Method" preparations

If you don't vote for me I'll hold my
breath.

> Posters put up by the supporters
> of SHIRLEY TEMPLE BLACK
> when she ran for office in California

I never vote for anyone. I always vote against.

W. C. Fields

I must say, it's the best bed-and-breakfast in America.

Tom Hanks, after he and his
wife stayed at the Clinton
White House

Anyone who works is a fool. I don't work—I merely inflict myself on the public.

Robert Morley

When I die, I have visions of fags singing "Over the Rainbow," and the flag at Fire Island being flown at half-mast.

JUDY GARLAND, well aware of
her huge gay following

I don't want to achieve immortality through my work. I want to achieve it through not dying.

WOODY ALLEN

It's our fault. We should have given him better parts.

Studio head JACK WARNER,
on hearing that RONALD
REAGAN had been elected
governor of California

No, Jimmy Stewart for President. Ronnie Reagan for best friend.

JACK WARNER again, when
Reagan first ran for President
in 1968

I'm not a right-wing jingoistic human being. Rambo is. He's psychotic in many ways.

SYLVESTER STALLONE

Boy, I saw *Rambo* last night. I know what to do next time this happens.

President RONALD REAGAN,
in June 1985, after the release
of thirty-nine American
hostages by Lebanese terrorists

The great nations have always acted like gangsters and the small nations like prostitutes.

STANLEY KUBRICK

Parboiled.

W. C. FIELDS, when asked how he liked children

Italian cat.

ANNA MAGNANI, when asked what kind of fur she was wearing at the 1956 Oscars

Everything you see, I owe to spaghetti.

SOPHIA LOREN

People think I have an interesting walk.
Hell, I'm just trying to hold my gut in.

ROBERT MITCHUM

And you coming back here and doing my
work is going to be just as foolish as my
going up and doing your personality with
that lousy fairy walk that you've got.

WILLIAM A. WELLMAN,
on star JOHN WAYNE's
interference when he was
directing *The High and the Mighty*

I'm not really Henry Fonda. Nobody could have that much integrity.

HENRY FONDA, on his image

Actually, I'm quite terrified of policemen; so much so that when I first came to America, I refused to drive a car, for fear a policeman would stop me and give me a ticket.

ALFRED HITCHCOCK

Everybody's in the elevator. It's a very crowded place.

HENRY MANCINI, responding to the charge that his songs and scores were just elevator music

I can pretty much kiss those Ibsen festivals good-bye.

JOHN GOODMAN, to JAY LENO,
on what playing Fred Flintstone
was likely to do for his career

I'm a whore. All actors are whores. We sell our bodies to the highest bidder.

WILLIAM HOLDEN

I was never interested in doing anything you can to make a lot of money. I didn't think of it. I was too dumb to be a whore. That takes hard work!

LENA HORNE, in 1994,
looking back

I don't want to do anything that makes me look even quasi-glamorous. I think it's absolute death for a comedian. I don't see myself as a romantic leading man at all. I just want to be funny.

DANA CARVEY, on the fact
that his role in *Clean Slate*
was originally developed for
ROBERT REDFORD

It's become very difficult to make a picture. Where are those butchers and scrap-iron dealers and illiterate giants now that we need them?

BILLY WILDER, in the 1960s,
on the tyrannical studio
moguls of the past

To me, bad taste is what entertainment is all about.

JOHN WATERS

We have a fax relationship. We draw really sick drawings and fax them to each other on our movie sets.

JODIE FOSTER, on how she
and her Maverick costar
MEL GIBSON keep in touch

Let's get a baby carriage, Ruthie, and you and I wheel it up South Water Street.

MIA FARROW, to RUTH GORDON
while visiting the latter at her home
in Edgartown, Massachusetts,
following the release of
Rosemary's Baby

It took about three days to film the scene because we got the giggles every time we heard it.

VINCENT PRICE, remembering
the famous scene in *The Fly*
in which he and HERBERT
MARSHALL discover the fly
with the tiny human head
weakly crying "Help" as it
lies trapped in a spiderweb

Paul Muni in *Seven Faces*—All Talking.

Hollywood theater marquee in 1929

It's a weird dichotomy. So many of us are shy, and then we end up becoming actors. We're shy exhibitionists.

GEENA DAVIS

People get into trouble trying to force themselves into adulthood. I'm still going to play whatever teenage roles I can. After all, I'll never be able to play those roles again.

LEONARDO DICAPRIO

I'm at the age where I've got to prove that I'm just as good as I never was.

REX HARRISON, in his sixties

I can't tell you how encouraging a thing like this is.

> RUTH GORDON, on winning the Best Supporting Actress Oscar at the age of seventy-two for *Rosemary's Baby*

Oh, Jim, weren't we beautiful then.

> AVA GARDNER, two weeks before her death in 1990, to her 1956 costar in *Bhowani Junction*, STEWART "JIM" GRANGER